W9-ACD-444

Plays to Ponder
for Grades 4-6

Prompting Classroom Discussion Through Dramatic Play

Written by Kimberly McCormick

Illustrated by Joan Holub

Dedication

For my sixth graders who inspired these plays, and my
entire family for their encouragement to keep writing.

Imprint Manager: Kristin Eclov

Senior Editor: Christine Hood

Inside and Cover Design: Jonathan Wu

Cover Illustration: Ken Bennett

GOOD APPLE

A Division of Frank Schaffer Publications, Inc.

23740 Hawthorne Boulevard

Torrance, CA 90505

Contents

Introduction

Today teachers play many roles. We are no longer "just teachers." We also play the roles of our students' advisors, parents, and friends. Our classrooms are filled with children who may be confused and needing advice about a variety of issues and problems, including organizing their school work, conflicts with siblings, and even experimenting with cigarettes and drugs. Seeing their needs every day in the classroom, and wanting to create an atmosphere in which students would feel comfortable facing and discussing these issues, I created **Plays to Ponder.** These short "skits" each introduce a topic dealing with an issue students face in their daily lives, and acts as a catalyst for discussion, journal writing, and a variety of "eye-opening" activities.

This book contains twenty plays presenting situations many young students face, including divorce, cheating on tests, good manners, and much more. The ideas for the plays came from my own students as we were studying theater and drama in my reading class. When I ran out of published plays, I went to my students for ideas. They wanted plays that were "real"—plays that dealt with situations they face on a day to day basis.

Plays to Ponder gives students a chance to not only deal with issues that are important to them, but also improve their oral presentation skills and self-esteem. You will be delighted to discover a shy, timid student may suddenly become an extrovert when placed in the role of a character. There's something about speaking in front of their peers that causes young people to lose their confidence. Yet, given the chance to speak in the role of a character, students will shine!

I use these plays in my classroom by having small student groups present assigned skits based on the topic of the day. I encourage students to memorize their lines and be prepared. If for some reason they are unable to memorize their lines, I ask them to at least be well-rehearsed. Normally, I spend a recess or study hall helping the group practice. When class begins, I announce the topic such as *Writing Notes During Class*. The group then presents their play for the class. Afterwards, I use follow-up discussion questions to encourage students to share their experiences, opinions, and ideas by relating to the characters in the play. Sometimes I have students participate in small-group discussions before having discussion as a class.

In addition to plays and discussion questions, this resource provides a variety of extension activities for each topic, inviting students to further explore and express themselves through writing, art, oral presentation, and interactive group projects. You may also want to have students keep running journals in which they can reflect on their personal feelings, behaviors, and experiences relating to each topic.

These plays can be used in any classroom as a way to break from the day's normal lessons to focus on a specific topic. For example, if you notice your class is having trouble getting their homework done on time, take some time to digress from the curriculum. Hold a theme day on organizing school work. Your students will enjoy the change of pace, and everyone is eager to have a turn presenting a play!

As teachers, we take responsibility for not only our students' educational well-being, but also play an important role in boosting their self-esteem and supporting their emotional health. **Plays to Ponder** provides an easy, fun, and interesting approach to opening the door for insightful classroom discussions. For many students, you may be the only adult willing to give your time to listen and talk about what is important to them. It is my hope that you and your students will enjoy and benefit from these plays as much as my students and I have.

Always Last

Topic: Choosing Teams for Games

After watching students choose teams at recess, I realized they needed to be more sensitive and considerate of others' feelings. This play helps students recognize the problems of choosing teams just by picking who they think is "best." It also prompts discussion on how to choose team members in ways that are fair and inclusive.

Characters: Doug*, Adam, Mando, Bill, Jae, and Troy
Holly*, Meg, Cherae, Rondi, Min, and Julie

*Holly and Doug are the only speaking parts.

Setting: School Playground

The students are selecting teams for a game of touch football. All but Doug and Holly are lined up side by side. While all parts except Holly and Doug are non-speaking, characters must remember to "react" to all dialogue, looking excited or disappointed as appropriate.

Holly: Come on, everyone. We have to get the teams picked. We're wasting our recess time just standing around talking.

Doug: Yeah, let's go. I want to get the game started.
Holly and I will be the captains. Holly, you can pick first.

Holly: Okay, then, I pick Min.

Students walk over to their captains as they are selected.

Doug: Mando.

Holly: Troy.

Doug: I'll take . . . Julie.

Holly: *(uncertainly, surveying her classmates who are watching her expectantly)*
Hmm . . . I guess I'll pick Rondi.

Doug   *(quickly)*
I want Bill.

Holly: Oh, Doug. I was just about to pick him!

Doug:	*(laughing)* Too bad!
Holly:	*(sighing)* Bill's good . . . Okay, then, I guess I'll take Meg.
Doug:	How about . . . Jae.
Holly:	Oh, no, you have to pick a girl now.
Doug:	Why?
Holly:	You know why! It's only fair. Girl, boy, girl, boy. That's how we always do it.
Doug:	Picky, picky. Okay, I forgot I just picked a guy. Okay . . . *(He looks at who's left with disappointment.)* I'll take . . . Cherae.
Holly:	Jae.
Doug:	Holly!
Holly:	What? It was my turn!
Doug:	Yeah, but you knew I was picking him next.
Holly:	Oh, well. *(She laughs, imitating Doug.)* Too bad!

There is silence for a moment, as Adam stands alone, looking uncomfortable.

Doug:	Well, I guess you're on my team then, Adam.

Adam walks slowly over to Doug's team. No one seems to notice that he feels bad. The other students laugh quietly.

Holly:	Let's go!

The students run offstage to play their game.

Always Last

Discussion Questions

- What procedure did these students use to pick teams? Is this how you usually choose teams for games? What's wrong with it?

- If you were a captain choosing teams, which would be more important to you—having your best friends on your team, or the best athletes? Explain your answer.

- Discuss two current philosophies now found in middle schools regarding team sports—a "no cut" policy and a "cut" policy. The idea behind the "no cut" policy is that all students will be included, and no one will feel left out— everyone is given a chance to play. The "cut" policy allows only the most qualified or skilled students to make the team. Should all interested students be permitted to play on a school's team? What do you think this "inclusive" policy would do to sports rankings and competition? Explain your answer.

- What does the following quote mean to you? *There is no such thing as a "star" of the team.*

- Even though a lot of people think winning is the most important thing about playing sports, there are lots of other reasons people play. Share reasons you or your friends play team sports. Also share other reasons you think playing team sports is a good way to develop responsibility, teamwork, cooperation, and good sportsmanship.

Extension Activities

- Invite students to write another skit from a different perspective—that of a child chosen last, like Adam. Adam could be talking to his mother, father, teacher, or friend about his experience. How might Adam feel about always being chosen last? This activity allows students to explore the situation from Adam's point of view.

- In small groups, invite students to come up with other ways students can pick teams without hurting anyone's feelings. For example, choosing names out of a hat, or forming teams using names in alphabetical order, and so on.

- Put student ideas into action by inviting them to play an indoor relay game! Have students choose teams using one of the methods they created in the above activity. If one method doesn't seem to work very well, move on to another. Try the following game, in which several teams can play at once.

"Pass the Eraser"

Place desks in straight rows. Each student passes a chalkboard eraser over his or her head to the person behind him or her. The last person in the row walks as fast as possible to the front desk, while all others move back a seat. Play continues until everyone is in his or her own seat.

Not Invited

Topic: Not Being Invited to a Party

I have a policy regarding party invitations in my classroom. It's either all the girls, all the boys, or everyone is invited. If someone wishes to have a smaller party, they must send invitations through the mail. This is my way of keeping children from getting hurt or feeling left out. In the following play, students discover what it feels like to be "left out." It also encourages them to devise ways they can include everybody in a party or other group activity in a fair and thoughtful way.

Characters: Sara, Chelsey, Mai, and Graciella (friends from school)

Setting: Classroom

Sara, Chelsey, and Mai are sitting at their desks talking before class begins.

Mai: I was thinking about going roller-skating Sunday afternoon. Do either of you think you could meet me there?

Sara: That would be fun! I'll check with my mom tonight.

Chelsey: I'm free. What time should we meet you?

Mai: Open skating starts at two o'clock and lasts until four-thirty. Try and get there a little bit early, because it gets really crowded now that they fixed the place up.

As the girls continue talking, Graciella walks up carrying several envelopes.

Graciella: Hey, everybody!

Mai: Hi, Graciella. What's up?

Graciella: Oh . . . I just have to give Sara and Chelsey something. Here you go.

Graciella hands both Sara and Chelsey an envelope, but gives Mai nothing.

Sara: What's this?

Graciella: Oh, it's just something I needed to give you. Open it later, okay?

Chelsey: Me too?

Graciella: Yeah, it's no big deal. Just open it later.

Sara:	Okay.
Graciella:	See you later.

Graciella goes back to her desk. When she's gone, the girls open up their envelopes.

Chelsey:	I can't wait until I get home to open this.
Sara:	Me neither. It's like waiting to open a Christmas present.
Mai:	What is it?
Sara:	*(She looks inside the envelope.)* Umm . . . Graciella was right, Mai. It's no big deal. *(She stuffs the invitation back into the envelope.)*
Chelsey:	Yeah, it's nothing. *(She starts to put her invitation away too, but Mai grabs it.)*
Mai:	It's an invitation to Graciella's birthday party. I guess I'm not invited. *(She looks more closely at the invitation.)* And it's on Sunday afternoon, right when we were going to go skating. Great.
Chelsey:	Maybe Graciella just forgot to invite you.
Mai:	Yeah, right. I was sitting right here when she gave them to you. That's why she told you not to open them until you got home. She was hoping I wouldn't find out.
Sara:	Well, maybe I could come skating for a while and go to Graciella's party later.
Chelsey:	It really wasn't very nice of Graciella to not invite you, Mai.
Mai:	Don't worry about it. Just go to her party. I'm really not surprised she didn't invite me. She's been mad at me ever since Mrs. Bryant picked me to help in the office instead of her.
Sara:	How dumb! All you do is run errands for the secretaries, right?
Mai:	Yeah, but I guess Graciella wanted to get out of class, and now she can't. It's not my fault, but she's taking it out on me.
Chelsey:	Don't feel bad, Mai. I'll probably go skating instead of to her party. That's a rotten thing for her to do to you.
Sara:	I'm sorry, Mai, but Graciella's party is at the miniature golf course, and I love to go golfing. I hope you're not mad if I go to the party.
Mai:	Whatever, Sara. Just do what you want. I'll have a good time skating even if both of you go to the party. I just wish Graciella would stop being so mean.

 GA1689

Not Invited

Discussion Questions

- If you were Chelsey or Sara, would you go to Graciella's party or skating with Mai? Do you feel Chelsey and Sara should have to choose between skating or Graciella's party? Share other solutions to the problem.

- How do you decide on who goes to your parties? How do you pass out invitations so that no one feels left out?

- What types of parties would allow everyone in the class to be included? (pool parties at the local YMCA, roller-skating, ice-skating, bowling, outdoor picnics)

- What are your favorite types of parties? Share one thing you like to do at these parties. Do you like to swim, play games, eat, tell stories?

Extension Activities

- Now is a great time to plan a classroom party! As a class, select a theme for your party (100th Day Celebration, St. Patrick's Day, First Day of Spring, Fall Festival, Parents' Day, and so on). Divide the class into small groups and assign various party-planning responsibilities such as games, decorations, invitations, food, and music. This will be a party to which everyone is invited and no one will feel left out!

- Create a classroom bulletin board of birthdays titled *Time for a Birthday Bash!* Give each student a bright-colored construction-paper balloon cutout. Have each student decorate the balloon by drawing his or her face on it or gluing on a photograph, then writing his or her name and birthday. Connect classroom balloons with yarn. Students with summer birthdays may list their "half" birthday. Give students a card signed by their classmates and a special treat on their special day.

- Experiment with creative writing! Tell students they have just received a party invitation to the "party of their dreams." Have each student create an invitation using construction paper and collage materials, then describe the party inside the card. After decorating the front of their cards, display the invitations for all to enjoy.

Pet Persuasion

Topic: Wanting a Pet

Nearly all children want a pet at one time or another, but they often don't realize the time and devotion that goes into caring for an animal. This play and the following discussion helps students to realize the responsibilities involved in pet care.

Characters: Bryan
His Mom and Dad

Setting: Pet Shop

Bryan and his parents are looking at a puppy in the pet-shop window.

Bryan: Look at the puppies!

Mom: Aww . . . they're so cute! I wonder what kind they are.

Bryan: They look like cocker spaniels.

Dad: I think that's what's what they are. They are cute, but don't get any bright ideas, Bryan.

Bryan: Dad! Can we ask if we can hold one? Please?

Dad: No, Bryan. We came to shop for school clothes, not a puppy.

Bryan: Dad, come on. I just want to hold one. The only pets I ever had were two fish. Big deal.

Mom: You wanted those fish, Bryan. We can't help it that you forgot to feed them and they died.

Bryan: I know, but fish are stupid. You can't pick them up; you can't play with them. What good are they? All you can do is sit and watch them swim!

Dad: I seem to remember someone who desperately wanted fish. He begged and begged his mother and father until he got them. Does that sound familiar?

Bryan: Yeah, but a dog is so much better. We could go on walks and play ball. He could even help protect the house. I'd love to have a dog.

Mom: Oh, look! That one puppy is jumping all over the other ones. Now he's coming over to the window. He's looking right at us.

GA1689

They all laugh.

Bryan: See what I mean? A fish never makes you laugh.

Dad: I understand what you're saying, Bryan, but I also remember the fish not being fed. What would happen to that little puppy if you forgot to feed it?

Bryan: How could I forget to feed a dog? Dogs are different. Please just ask them to take the puppy out so we can hold him.

Dad: I don't think that's such a good idea.

Bryan: I know you like dogs, Dad. It would be so much fun!

Mom: I'm afraid your dad is right. I'm not sure you're ready to handle the responsibility of a puppy. They're a lot of work.

Bryan: I'll do anything, Mom. What do you want me to do to prove to you that I can take care of a puppy?

Mom: I don't know.
(She looks at her husband.)
Do you have any ideas? After seeing those fish belly-up in the aquarium, I don't know if I'm ready for another pet.

Bryan: Most of my friends have pets. Their parents all seem to think they're responsible enough to take care of them.

Dad: I understand what you're saying, and I think it would be great to have a dog. But first you're going to have to prove that you're going to be responsible. If you can think of some way to earn our trust back, then we'll talk about getting a puppy, okay?

Bryan: Okay. Just tell me what to do.

Dad: We'll put our heads together and think of something.

Bryan: Really?

Dad: Just remember what I said.

Bryan: I promise.

Mom: Come on, we don't have all day to spend at the pet store. Let's go get some clothes.

They walk away as Bryan looks over his shoulder longingly at the puppy.

Pet Persuasion

Discussion Questions

- How can Bryan prove to his parents that he's responsible enough to care for a dog?

- Today's ever-popular Giga Pets™ were designed for children to prove that they can be responsible with pets. Giga Pets™ act as "simulated pets" that need care, attention, food, and so on. If Giga Pet™ owners neglect to care for their pets properly, they will "die." How do you feel taking care of Giga Pets™ compares to caring for real pets?

- For those of you who have pets, share how much time each day (or week) you spend taking care of them (include feeding, washing, cleaning up, grooming, and so on). What are some of the daily tasks you perform in caring for your pets? Do the responsibilities differ according to the animal? Explain.

- What are the pros and cons of pet ownership? Dogs can be good friends, sleep with you at night, go to the park with you, and help protect the house. Dogs can also cost a lot of money—vet bills, grooming, and food. They must be trained, need lots of attention, and can be messy.

- Do you have any idea how much it costs to own a dog? cat? horse? Estimate how much money you think it costs to care for several different animals.

Extension Activities

- As a class, develop weekly schedules or graphs of the time it takes to care for various animals (e.g., fish, hamster, cat, dog, rabbit, bird, horse). Include feeding, grooming, bathing, exercise and play time, and so on. When schedules are complete, invite students to compare and contrast the time needed to care for each animal. Ask students to share which animals they think they could care for, and those they think would be too time consuming. Children can also graph the costs of caring for different animals.

- Have children draw pictures or bring in photographs of their pets, and write a paragraph sharing a funny story. For students who don't have pets, invite them to draw a pet they would like to have, or share a favorite pet of a friend or relative.

- Honor pets with special rewards and titles! Ask students to select favorite pictures of their pets (or pets they would like to have). Next, ask them to write a paragraph describing what title their pet should win, such as "World's Funniest Dog" or "America's Craziest Cat." Place animal pictures with their titles on a bulletin-board display for all to enjoy. Title your display *Award-Winning Pets!* or *And the Award Goes to . . . .*

- Invite students to take home a class pet to learn about the real responsibilities of pet care. First, send home a parent letter describing the activity, and then send home a hamster, rabbit, or guinea pig. Ask each student to keep the animal at home for a week and record in a journal what steps they take each day to care for the "pet." After all students have taken home the animal, invite them to share their notes with the class. They may be surprised to discover how much time and effort it takes to properly care for a pet!

Bedtime? You've Got to Be Kidding!

> ## Topic: Bedtime
>
> *Children are always looking for ways to make their bedtime later. They often view a later bedtime as a sign that they are getting older and can be trusted with more responsibility. This play explores the "struggle" between parents and children regarding bedtime, and how much sleep children really need to stay healthy and alert.*

Characters: Sam (age 11) and Elsa (age 9); brother and sister
Their Mom and Dad

Setting: Living Room

Sam, Elsa, and their dad are watching television. Mom walks in and announces that it's time for Sam and Elsa to go to bed.

Mom: Hey, kids, it was bedtime half an hour ago. Let's go.

Sam: Mom! The movie is going to be over in ten minutes, and it's the best part. Can't we stay up just ten more minutes?

Elsa: Please, Mom?

Dad: It sounds to me like you've already stayed up past your bedtime.
Your mother said to go to bed, so get going.

Sam: But, Dad, this is not fair! I'm two years older than Elsa, and I still have the same bedtime. I've had the same bedtime for five years! Don't you think it's time we changed it?

Elsa: Wait a minute. Just because you're two years older doesn't mean you should get to stay up later than me.

Sam: Why not? There should be some advantage to being the oldest. I mean, I usually have to take the blame for everything just because I'm older.

Mom: Wait just a minute. We're discussing bedtime. That's all. And I say you kids need to go to bed—now!

Elsa: But I'm not even tired!

Sam: Me neither!

Mom:	Then why are you both so grumpy in the morning? I have to practically drag you out of bed. Then by the time you eat your breakfast and get your teeth brushed, the bus is outside honking the horn. You both need to be in bed.
Sam:	Mom! It's still light out!
Elsa:	Yeah, can't we at least stay up until the sun goes down?
Dad:	Both of you to bed—now!
Sam:	Can't we at least have a snack before we go to bed? I'm really hungry, and I can't sleep on an empty stomach.
Elsa:	I know, I'm starving, Mom. Please?
Sam:	And I still need to brush my teeth.
Elsa:	Me too.
Dad:	This isn't up for debate. Go brush your teeth, and get into bed.
Sam:	Just fifteen more minutes . . .
Mom:	*(throwing her hands in the air)* Ahhhh! Quit arguing with me and just GO TO BED!

Sam and Elsa plug their ears and run out. After a moment of silence, Sam and Elsa both yell from offstage at the same time.

Sam/Elsa:	We're in bed!

Dad looks at Mom and laughs, but Mom doesn't think it's funny.

Mom:	I'm really getting sick of this every night.
Dad:	*(calling to Sam and Elsa)* Get up and brush your teeth!

Mom collapses into a chair. Dad just smiles and goes back to watching television, while Mom lies down to rest.

Bedtime? You've Got to Be Kidding!

Discussion Questions

• Does this scene sound familiar? Does this happen often in your own home?

• Do you have a set bedtime? Is it different during the week and on the weekends? Why do you think this is?

• Do you try nearly every night to stay up later than your bedtime? What kind of excuses do you use for wanting to stay up later?

• How do you feel about Sam and Elsa having the same bedtime? Do you think Sam makes a valid point that being two years older should allow him a later bedtime? If yes, why do you think Sam is grumpy and hard to wake up in the morning?

• What are some ways Sam could demonstrate to his parents that he's ready for a later bedtime? If you've had your bedtime moved to a later time, how did you convince your parents to change it? Has it worked for you?

Extension Activities

• Studies tell us we can learn how many hours of sleep we need by checking what time we wake up naturally, without an alarm clock. Over several days, have students notice the pattern of how many hours they sleep before waking up. When they have close to the same results for a few days, this number is most likely how many hours of sleep their bodies require each night. The average number of hours people need to sleep varies greatly from one person to the next. Tell students to find out what's right for them and stick to it! They will be happier, healthier, and full of energy! (This activity may be easier completed over spring or winter break, or over several weekends when children don't have to get up for school.)

• Everyone loves to share their dreams. Divide your class into small groups and ask students to share one of their funniest, most interesting, or most bizarre dreams with classmates. Ask them to choose their favorite dream to role-play for the class. You may also want to use this activity as a pre-writing strategy. After verbally sharing their dreams, invite students to write about and illustrate them, creating a classroom "Book of Dreams" for everyone to enjoy.

• Ask students to keep a "Sleep Log" for one week. They should include the time they go to bed and the time they wake up each day. They should also record any naps they may take during the week. When the week is up, students can share results with classmates. Have them compare and contrast the amount of sleep they get, their bedtimes, and whether or not these schedules keep them feeling alert and awake or tired throughout the week. This is a good opportunity for students to learn from each other.

• Invite students to research various sleep phenomena and disorders, such as insomnia, sleep apnea, dreams, sleepwalking, snoring, talking in one's sleep, night terrors, and so on. Ask student groups to each research one topic and then share their findings with the class through a short written report or an oral presentation.

More Chores?

Topic: Helping with Chores Around the House

As children grow up, their responsibilities increase as well. Being part of a family includes sharing in chores and responsibilities around the home. This play helps students realize how much their parents and other family members do for them, and how helping in even little ways (without complaining!) is so much appreciated by others.

Characters: Devon (age 12) and Kyra (age 10); brother and sister
                       Their Mom

Setting: Living Room

Devon and Kyra are sprawled out in front of the television when Mom comes in. She is drying a dish with a dish towel.

Mom: I'd appreciate it if one of you would come into the kitchen and help me with the dishes, please.

Kyra: This movie is over in half an hour, okay, Mom?

Mom: No, it is not okay. I would like you to help me now, please.

Kyra: I'll miss the end of the movie! Have Devon do it.

Devon: *(throwing a pillow at Kyra)*
Yeah, right! I'm not doing the dishes. That's a girl's job.

Mom: There is no such thing. A chore is a chore.

Kyra: *(throwing the pillow back at Devon)*
I bet you would let the dishes pile up to the ceiling before you would help!

Devon: *(laughing)*
Probably.

Kyra: You're so gross!

Mom: It seems to me, Kyra, that you're not much better. I'm in this kitchen night after night, by myself, washing and drying the dishes. I've had it!

Mom leaves the room.

Devon: Why is Mom so mad?

Kyra: I don't know. Did we say something wrong?

Devon: I don't think so. Oh, well, let's finish watching the movie.

Devon and Kyra turn back to the TV. Mom walks back in writing on a notepad. She then goes to the TV and shuts it off. Devon and Kyra cry out in protest.

Mom: Devon . . . Kyra. As I already said, I've had it. First, I asked both of you nicely to give me some help. But now, I'm telling you to help me. Here are both of your new lists of chores.

With a smile, Mom hands both children a piece of paper.

Mom: Get busy!

Kyra: Mom, this isn't fair!

Devon: Come on, Mom, we just wanted to finish watching the movie.

Mom: You're both plenty old enough to help out with the chores. There's only the three of us here, and I work long hours all week. You'll be pleased to see the number-one priority on your list of chores, Devon.

Devon looks at his list.

Devon: Washing and drying the dishes! Mom!

Mom and Kyra laugh a little.

Kyra: That's a good one, Mom!

Mom: You have a list there, too, Kyra.

Kyra looks at her list.

Kyra: Pull weeds!

Mom: There's a lot of things to take care of around here, and I can't do it all.

Kyra: Okay, okay. I'm sorry. I realize how much work you have to do. I'll try and be more helpful.

Mom: Thank you, Kyra.

Kyra: Come on, Devon. I'll dry if you wash.

Devon: *(dragging his feet and mumbling)*
Yeah, yeah, yeah. But I still think doing dishes is a girl's job.

More Chores?

Discussion Questions

- Do your parents give you chores to do each week? Do you think it's fair? Why do you think your parents ask you to help around the house? Do you complain about having to do chores?

- Are there some chores you consider to be a "boy's job" or a "girl's job"? Why?

- If you had to pick a "favorite chore," what would it be, and why?

- Think of all the responsibilities your parents handle every day. Do you think they have a hard time balancing work and home responsibilities? What are some ways you could "pitch in" to make their lives easier?

- In what ways can you make chores more fun or rewarding?

Extension Activities

- Have children list the jobs for which they are responsible at home. Ask them to check off those jobs they think are unfair or too burdensome. Then ask them to write another list of all the jobs/chores for which their parents/guardians are responsible. This list will be much longer. (If children aren't sure of all their parents' responsibilities, you may have them make this second list as a homework assignment.) After both lists are complete, ask students if they still think their chores are unfair, and why. Invite them to share if there are chores or jobs on their parents' lists with which they could help out.

- Work Wanted! Ask students to write their own classified ad or flyer describing the types of chores they enjoy (e.g., washing cars, working in the garden). Invite them to write persuasively, including why they are good at this task, why they enjoy it, and why someone should "hire" them. Students may wish to distribute their ads to their parents or close neighbors. This may be a great way for students to earn some extra money!

- Invite students to do some creative writing! Have them write and illustrate "want ads" convincing others to want to do particularly tedious or "gross" chores. Distribute examples of advertisements from magazines and newspapers, and discuss the various tactics advertisers use to persuade consumers to buy their products. Have a contest to see who can make chores such as cleaning toilets or scrubbing pots and pans the most adventuresome, fun, or intriguing!

19

GA1689

The Dog Ate My Homework

Topic: Planning for and Organizing School Work

Is your class having trouble getting their homework done on time? Are they having problems organizing daily assignments? Use this play as a springboard for discussion on organization, planning, and study skills, and help students get back on track!

Characters: Mr. Lemmon (teacher)
Kirstin (student in Mr. Lemmon's class)
Several other students (non-speaking parts)

Setting: Mr. Lemmon's Classroom

As students get ready for class, Kirstin frantically searches through her papers for her homework. Mr. Lemmon enters the room.

Kirstin: *(mumbling to herself)*
I can't find my homework! I did it, I swear I did. Mr. Lemmon is never going to believe me. Where is it?

Mr. Lemmon: All right, class, please take out last night's homework.

All the students take out their papers. Kirstin places a paper on her desk, too.

Mr. Lemmon: I'll just take a quick walk around the room to see that everyone has their work done. Just sit patiently for a minute.

Mr. Lemmon walks around the class, looking on each student's desk. He stops by Kirstin and examines her paper closely.

Mr. Lemmon: Kirstin, this is yesterday's work. Where is your homework for today?

Kirstin: I can't find it, Mr. Lemmon. But I swear I did it.

Mr. Lemmon: You may have done it, Kirstin, but the fact is, you need it with you right now to earn credit for it. I guess you'll have to stay in at recess and do it again.

Kirstin: Can't I just have a few more minutes to look for it? I'm sure I stuck it in my notebook somewhere. It's probably just mixed in with the wrong papers or something.

Mr. Lemmon: You may have a minute while I continue checking the rest of the class. I'll come back to you.

As Mr. Lemmon continues to look at other students' papers, Kirstin continues searching through her messy notebook. Papers are everywhere. She is obviously very unorganized. Mr. Lemmon returns to Kirstin's desk when he's finished.

Mr. Lemmon: Well, Kirstin, any luck?

Kirstin: No.

Mr. Lemmon: Then I'm sorry, but I can't give you any credit.

Kirstin: That doesn't seem fair, Mr. Lemmon. You can even call my mother. She knows I did this homework!

Mr. Lemmon: As I already said Kirstin, I'm very sorry, but you need your homework right now, and you don't seem to have it. You have to learn to be responsible for your own work.

Kirstin: Can I maybe make it up?

Mr. Lemmon thinks a minute.

Mr. Lemmon: Okay, why don't you come in at recess and do the assignment over again. But I won't be so understanding next time.

Kirstin: Thank you, Mr. Lemmon.

Mr. Lemmon: Maybe after school we can take a minute to organize your notebook. That might help. What do you think?

Kirstin: Oh, I know where everything is, Mr. Lemmon. My notebook's pretty neat compared to how I usually keep it.

The other students laugh.

Student: Yeah, Mr. Lemmon, you should see inside Kirstin's desk! *(laughter)*

Mr. Lemmon: *(laughing)*
I think I'm afraid to. Seriously, Kirstin, I'd be glad to help you. If you would just keep all your papers together by subject, it'd be a lot easier to keep them organized.

Kirstin: *(somewhat grudgingly)*
Okay, I'll stay after school so you can help me get organized.

Mr. Lemmon: Great! But remember, you still have that homework to do as well.—Anyone else who's interested in learning how to organize your school work can stay after class. Now, hand your papers to the front of your rows so we can get started. We have a lot of things to cover today.

The Dog Ate My Homework

Discussion Questions

- How do you feel Mr. Lemmon should handle the situation of Kirstin not having her homework?

- Why do you feel teachers assign homework? Do you think they assign too much? too little?

- How much homework do you feel is a fair amount to have each night? As you get older, should you receive more homework?

- Should you be rewarded for doing your homework? Should there be an incentive for completing homework and a consequence when you don't? What excuses do you believe are important enough to excuse you from not having your homework?

- How do you organize your school work? Share some of the ways you organize, study, and plan for long- and short-term assignments.

Extension Activities

- Give your students a step-by-step lesson on how to organize. Suggest keeping subjects separated in different parts of a large notebook, or in different folders. Color-coding is also an effective way to differentiate between subjects. Encourage them to keep daily lists of assignments. Copy an "Assignments for the Day" sheet, and complete it together as a class. Make this a daily requirement for students, and check their sheets at the end of each day.

- Excuses! Excuses! Students will have fun working with their classmates to create the "World's Greatest No-Homework Excuses." Laugh together as students share the best and worst excuses they can think of as to why they don't have their homework ready. You may also want to share some of the excuses you've heard from students over the years!

- Most students don't know how to properly plan out and organize their time and school work. Sometimes just being unorganized can hinder students from doing well in school. Help them implement basic time management and organizational skills and strategies by following these suggestions from *Helping Kids Get Organized* by Robyn Freedman Spizman and Marianne Daniels Garber, Ph.D. (Good Apple, 1995).

1. *Organize Your Environment*—Find a place to study that is away from noise and other distractions (TV, radio, telephones, siblings, pets). Make sure it's well lit and "stocked" with study tools.

2. *Identify and Use the Correct Study Tools*—There are a variety of items that help you study, i.e., pencils, pens, erasers, computer, paper, calculator, encyclopedias, dictionary, index cards, thesaurus, ruler, file folders, filing cabinet or box, and calendar. Make a list of these items and check off those you have at home.

3. *Develop Effective Homework Habits*—Set up a "homework routine," in which you study at the same time each day. Take occasional breaks to give your mind a rest, and leave your homework in a special place so you don't forget to bring it to school!

4. *Work Efficiently with Deadlines*—This is a hard one! Most students often feel overwhelmed by multiple projects and assignments. Make lists of all the things you have to do, and then prioritize them. Breaking projects down into smaller, prioritized tasks will help you meet your deadlines and set the proper priorities. With large reading assignments, break the reading down into several pages per day. You may also want to keep weekly assignment sheets for each subject.

5. *Properly Prepare for Tests*—When preparing for a test, find out what kind of test it is (short answer, true/false, multiple choice) and exactly what will be covered, so you will know what information you need to review.

Too Much TV!

> ## Topic: Finding Alternatives to Television
>
> *Students love to watch and talk about television. Unfortunately, many children spend hours planted in front of the TV each day. But how much TV is too much? This play prompts student to explore their television-watching habits, and devise other ways they can spend their time more productively.*

Characters: Mia and Steph (neighborhood friends)
Steph's Mom

Setting: Steph's Bedroom

Mia and Steph are watching the television in Steph's bedroom.

Mia: This is the best game show on television. I never miss it.

Steph: I know. Actually, I like the one that comes on before this one better.

Mia: It is so great to be out of school. I could lie around and watch TV all day. My Mom was yelling at me about it earlier this morning. That's one reason why I wanted to come over here. She threatened to turn the TV off, and I would have missed this show!

Steph: You don't have to worry about that here. Usually my mom doesn't bother me about it. As long as I'm not getting into trouble, she doesn't care if I watch TV all day long.

Mia: You are so lucky. Are you allowed to stay up late watching TV, too?

Steph: During the summer I am. And I love having a TV in my room. Then my brother and I don't fight over what to watch.

Mia: That will never happen at my house. I'm lucky if I get to watch an hour a day. You have it made!

As the girls continue watching TV, Steph's mom peeks her head in the door.

Mom: Steph, are you girls watching TV?

Steph: Yeah, why?

Mom: Well, Mia, I just got off the phone with your mother, and she asked that I tell you to go home if you're over here watching TV.

Mia: You've got to be kidding! I can't believe this! How embarrassing.

Mom: I have to admit, Steph, Mia's mother made a lot of sense.

Steph: What did she say?

Mom: She feels that on such a nice summer day you girls should be outside riding bikes, or swimming, or just taking a walk and enjoying the outdoors. Why don't you two go do something outside?

Steph: Mom! You never care if I watch TV!

Mom: I know, but like I said, Mia's mom has a good point. You girls need to get more exercise. It's unhealthy spending so much time just sitting and watching show after show.

Mia: My mom makes me so mad!

Mom: Don't feel that way, Mia. Your mom called because she cares about you. That's why she doesn't want you wasting your time in front of the TV all day. Come on, what do you two say about going to the park? I have some free time, and I could drive you there. Maybe we could walk the trails together.

Steph: Mom, we really wanted to watch this show.

Mom: Well, we either decide what activity you two can do, or Mia has to go home. I guess it's up to you.

Mia: Come on, Steph. It's a losing battle with my mom. I told you how she feels about this. I think we better take your mom up on her offer, unless, of course, you'd rather watch this game show. I can go home.

Steph: I'm sure, Mia. Let's just go to the park. Mom, when we get there, do you think we could go swimming?

Mom: I think that's a great idea. Maybe we could try doing a little trip each week this summer. What do you think about that?

Steph: That would be fun.

Mia: I'm sure that would make my mom happy, too.

The girls pretend to get ready to go to the park. As the scene closes, the girls toss around ideas of other fun activities they may choose to do in the future, such as having a picnic or playing tennis.

Too Much TV!

Discussion Questions

● Share your feelings and opinions about watching television. When do you consider television a good activity? When do you feel it is a waste of time?

● Do you ever watch TV just because you're bored? What other activities could you do rather than watching television?

● Are there any shows your family watches together? Share them with the class. Why do you think these make good family shows? Are there any shows you are not allowed to watch? What are they, and why aren't you allowed to watch them?

● What is your favorite television show? What activity do you enjoy doing so much that you would be willing to give up this show?

● Do you feel television can affect your moods? How? Do you believe that violence on television influences people's behavior? If yes, why do you think so?

Extension Activities

● Ask each student to complete a television-viewing chart for one week. Have students record what shows they watch, the times, and total viewing hours for each day. At the end of the week, calculate a grand total of television viewing hours for the class. Figure out the class average for each day of the week and ask students to graph the results. You may even want to figure out how much TV students watch in one month and one year. Students will be amazed at how much time they "waste" in front of the TV!

● Divide the class into small groups, and ask each group to brainstorm a list of activities they enjoy other than watching television. Then come together as a class and create a classroom list of ideas. Invite students to copy these down for times they feel bored and are tempted to just "plop down" in front of the TV.

● Select one week of the year in which the class agrees to try and cut back on or totally cut out watching television. Invite students to keep a journal all week describing the new and/or interesting activities they did instead. At the end of the week, invite students to share their journals with classmates. Have students use these ideas to create a class book of "alternatives to television."

● Invite students to write TV show reviews like the experts do! Have them begin their review with one descriptive word such as *boring, exciting,* or *funny,* then write a brief review citing reasons for their opinion. Have them add what they believe to be the best and worst aspects of the show, and talk about the characters as well. Then, invite them to share reasons why, or why not, their classmates should, or shouldn't, watch this show. Finally, invite students to rate the show on a scale of one to ten or with a five-star system.

Just One?

Topic: Experimenting with Cigarettes

Your students are at the age when they will be faced with various peer-pressure situations, including cigarette smoking and drugs. This play will promote discussion about peer pressure, and how important it is to have "all the facts" about substance abuse.

Characters: Jason, Gilbert, Ashley, and Ana (neighborhood friends)

Setting: Behind Jason's Garage

The four kids are looking for something to do on a rather boring, hot summer day.

Ashley: What do you guys want to do?

Gilbert: We could find some other kids to play softball.

Jason: No, we just played yesterday. I'm sick of softball.

Ana: Well, let's get our bikes out and ride down to the store. I've got some money. We could get something to eat or go to the video store.

Gilbert: My bike has a flat. Sorry.

Ashley: I'm so bored! We have to think of something to do!

Jason: *(pulling a small box from his pocket)*
I have an idea.

Gilbert: What's that?

Ana: Jason! Are those cigarettes? Where did you get them?

Jason: Shhhh! Quit being so loud! Do you want my dad to hear?

Ana: *(whispering)*
All right, where did you get them?

Jason: Out of my dad's truck. He'll never know the difference. He has packs of cigarettes in every room of the house.

Ashley: Well, what do you plan to do with them? You're not going to smoke them, are you?

GA1689

Gilbert: I'll try one. There's nothing else better to do. I guess just one isn't a big deal. *(He takes a cigarette from Jason.)*

Jason offers a cigarette to the girls, but they just shake their heads.

Jason: Let's see who can blow a smoke ring.

Gilbert: I'll bet I can blow smoke out of my nose.

Ashley: *(laughing)*
You're so gross!

Ana: I don't know, Jason. My mom and dad don't smoke, and they always tell me how bad it is for you.

Jason: That's stupid, Ana. My mom and dad and my grandparents have all smoked since they were teenagers. They look fine to me.

Ashley: You only see what's on the outside, Jason. Maybe on the inside they're not so fine.

Jason: *(defensively)*
There's nothing wrong with anyone in my family, even if they do smoke.

Ashley: I'm sorry, Jason. I wasn't trying to make you mad. I just don't want Ana to think it's okay to smoke, because it's not.

Gilbert: Well, I'm with you, Jason. We don't need the girls around anyway.

Jason: That's right. Why don't both of you go ride your bikes. We'll have more fun here by ourselves.

Ana: That's fine with me. Do you want to go bike riding, Ashley?

Ashley: Yeah, let's go. I'm sorry you guys, but that smoke is going to make my clothes stink.

Jason laughs.

Jason: What are you afraid of?

Ashley: I'm not afraid, I just think cigarettes smell. Come on Ana, let's go.

Ana: Sorry, you guys.

Jason: Whatever.

Ana and Ashley walk off together, while Jason and Gilbert begin to smoke the cigarettes.

GA1689

Just One?

Discussion Questions

- Why do you think so many people continue to smoke when they know cigarettes have been proven to be dangerous to their health?

- What is second-hand smoke? Do you think second-hand smoke is dangerous? How do you react to being in the situation of breathing in second-hand smoke?

- It sounds easy to "just say no," but when you're afraid of being excluded for not "going along," it's difficult to say no. If your friends were pressuring you to smoke, how would you handle the situation?

- Recently, many people have been awarded huge sums of money from cigarette companies. These people claim the companies falsely advertised their product and sold cigarettes knowing they could cause serious health problems. Do you agree or disagree with these decisions? Why? Should people be held responsible for smoking or should the tobacco companies?

- On billboards and in magazines, beautiful women and handsome men appear in cigarette advertisements. Also, Joe Camel continues to be a popular figure promoting cigarettes, especially with younger smokers. Why do you think cigarette companies use these types of characters in their ads? What do you think they're trying to say about smoking cigarettes?

Extension Activities

- In small groups, have students brainstorm all the reasons they can think of to smoke and then why NOT to smoke. Ask them to share and discuss their lists with the class.

- Incorporate a math lesson into your discussion! Tell students the current cost of a pack of cigarettes. Ask them to calculate how much money it would cost if a person smoked a pack of cigarettes a day for one week, for one month, and for one year. Discuss how smoking is not only unhealthy, it's also expensive! Ask students what else they could do with the money they would save by not smoking.

- Invite students to design clever, catchy posters that promote the benefits of not smoking. Encourage them to use advertising techniques they see in cigarette ads as a way of promoting a "cigarette free" environment. Display students' finished posters around the school.

- Ask students to take a poll on cigarette smoking. Have them ask other students and adults if they smoke, then ask them why they do or do not smoke. After a week of surveying, have students share their results with the class. Did students find commonalities in the responses they received?

Manners Matter

Topic: Using Good Manners

Nothing impresses people more than someone with good manners. Good manners demonstrate good upbringing, self-respect, as well as respect for others. This play promotes discussion of not only the good manners we show in social situations, but also how we can show respect and good manners at home.

Characters: Jayna (age 12) and Alex (age 10); brother and sister
Mr. and Mrs. Burpee (their parents)

Setting: The Burpee Living Room

Mr. Burpee plops down in a chair and opens up his newspaper. He opens a bag of pretzels and begins to eat, smacking loudly, with his mouth open.

Mr. Burpee: Ahhh, time to relax. Alex, go get my slippers.

Alex just looks at his dad. Mr. Burpee throws a pretzel at him.

Mr. Burpee: I said, get my slippers.

Alex gets the slippers and brings them to his dad. He waits for a moment.

Alex: Well, aren't you going to say something?

Mr. Burpee: Yeah, next time get them for me the first time I ask. Jayna, go get me a soda.

Jayna: Okay, Dad. Can I please just see the end of this show? It's ending right now.

Mr. Burpee: I'm thirsty now, not five minutes from now. Come on, let's go.

Jayna goes into the kitchen and comes back with a soda for her father. Mr. Burpee takes a swallow and lets out a loud belch.

Mr. Burpee: Ahhh, I feel much better.
(*Alex laughs behind his hand, and Jayna gives her father a disgusted look.*)
You know what they say, Jayna, better out than in.

Jayna: That's really gross, Dad.

Mrs. Burpee: Honey, would you please excuse yourself when you do that?

Mr. Burpee: What for? It's a natural bodily function. If I can't relax at home, where can I?

Alex: Better out than in, Mom.

Mr. Burpee: That's my boy. Now you're learning.

Alex: Yeah, I'm learning.
(whispering to Jayna)
I'm learning what *not* to be like when I grow up.

Mrs. Burpee: I think supper is just about ready. Do you all want to come to the table?

Mr. Burpee: Just bring me a tray in here. I want to finish watching the game.

Mrs. Burpee: I was hoping we could share a family meal together. Won't you come to the table and eat with the rest of us?

Mr. Burpee: Not tonight, hon. Just bring my food in here. I can't miss this game; it's the play-offs. Go ahead and eat together if you want.

Jayna: *(quietly to Alex)*
I don't know how Mom puts up with him sometimes.

Alex: He's not so bad.

Mr. Burpee lets loose with a loud sneeze, then wipes his nose on his sleeve and continues watching television, oblivious to his poor manners.

Mrs. Burpee: *(handing Mr. Burpee a tissue)*
Here's a tissue, dear.

Mr. Burpee: That's okay. I took care of it.

Jayna: *(whispering to Alex)*
I don't know how we ever learned manners at all.

While they are talking, Mr. Burpee falls asleep. Everyone is startled by his loud snoring.

Jayna: He snores so loud! How do you ever sleep with him, Mom?
Does he always snore like that?

Mrs. Burpee: I guess he does. I must be used to it by now, but somebody needs to teach him some manners. I've given up. Well, let's go eat.

Alex: How come we always have to say "please" and "thank-you" and Dad doesn't?

Jayna: Good question.

Mrs. Burpee: Because you two have good manners, that's why. Maybe we can come up with a plan to teach your father some manners over supper. Let's go.

Mrs. Burpee, Alex, and Jayna walk into the dining room while Mr. Burpee continues snoring loudly.

Manners Matter

Discussion Questions

- Discuss how though the skit was humorous and far-fetched, it demonstrates the importance of good manners, whether in a social situation or at home with your family. Lots of people have good manners when they're out in public, but then forget to show respect for the people they live with, as Mr. Burpee demonstrates so well.

- What were some of the poor manners Mr. Burpee demonstrated? How else might he have handled himself in a more mannerly way?

- Do your manners change when you are out in public as compared to at home? Should they? Do you feel the same respect should be given to your immediate family as to your teachers, friends, and strangers?

- How do you feel manners make a good first impression when you meet others, such as referring to adults by their last names, or with "sir" or "ma'am."

- What manners are important in your house? How have you always been taught to behave in public and at home? Which manners do you feel are the most important to always use?

- Do you know how manners may change from one country to another? (Burping at the table in our country may be distasteful and rude, yet it is a sign of the meal being delicious in others. In some countries it is impolite to meet someone else's eyes or smile at them; looking down is a sign of respect.)

- Men in our country have always been taught certain manners about how to act around women, such as holding the door for them, a "ladies first" policy, paying the bill, and so on. Do you feel these manners are still appropriate? If you could change these "expectations," how would you change them?

Women have also been taught certain manners regarding men, such as not voicing their opinions as strenuously as men, letting men win at games or sports, and so on. How have times changed? How have they stayed the same?

Extension Activities

- Invite student groups to write skits showing various situations in which good manners are important. Skits can be serious, funny, real, or made up. Have students present these situations to the class, and then invite their classmates to respond with which manners should be used. Some suggestions include:

  - answering the telephone and taking a message
  - introducing your friend or parent to another person he or she has never met
  - meeting someone's parents for the first time
  - buying something at a market or clothing store
  - having supper at a friend's house

- Help students become aware of their manners by creating a "Manners Chart" that lists several commonly-used phrases such as *please, thank you, excuse me, pardon, sir/ma'am*, and so on. For one day, each time they hear themselves use these phrases, students can make a checkmark beside the phrase on their charts. The next day, have students share their results with the class.

May I ask who's calling, please?

To Cheat or Not to Cheat: That Is the Question

Topic: Cheating on a Test

Probably all of us have been tempted to cheat at one time or another—on an important test, a surprise quiz we're unprepared for, in a race, game, and so on. This play helps students look at cheating, and why it is more rewarding in the long run to just simply do your best.

Characters: Jennifer and Michael (classmates)
Ms. Davis (their teacher)
Several other students (non-speaking parts)

Setting: Ms. Davis's Classroom

Jennifer and Michael are studying together before a geography test.

Jennifer: What is the capital of Pennsylvania?

Michael: Ummm . . . Erie?

Jennifer: No, Harrisburg. Name the Great Lakes.

Michael: Oh, I know this one. That's easy. Erie, Michigan, Huron, Conneaut, and . . .

Jennifer: Wrong. Michael, did you study?

Michael: I tried, but my sister and her friends were having a party at my house last night. It was so noisy I couldn't even concentrate. Obviously, I'm going to fail.

Jennifer: I'm sorry. Why didn't your parents make your sister and her friends be quiet?

Michael: They weren't home. As soon as they left, she invited all her friends over. She was in so much trouble when my parents got home. Not that that helps me today. What am I going to do?

Jennifer: Well, normally I wouldn't offer to do this, but I feel bad for you. If you're really careful, I'll try to leave my paper open so you can see some of my answers, okay? Just don't get caught, because then we'll both get in trouble.

Michael: Thanks. I owe you one.

Ms. Davis calls the class to attention.

Ms. Davis: Okay, class. That's enough time to go over your notes. Put your books and notes away. It's time to take the test.

Ms. Davis passes out the tests. All the students then turn over their papers and begin. After a minute or two, Jennifer moves her arm out of the way and pushes her paper to the side of her desk so Michael can glance at it if he chooses. Michael takes a quick glance.

Ms. Davis: I think I see some roving eyes. I hope we will all do our own work.

Michael looks quickly back to his own paper. After a while, he looks at Jennifer's paper again.

Ms. Davis: Michael, will you please bring your test to me?

Jennifer gives Michael an alarmed look as he brings his test to Ms. Davis's desk.

Ms. Davis: *(quietly, so only Michael can hear)*
I tried to be nice and give you a warning, but you are continuing to look at Jennifer's paper. I'm going to have to fail you.

Michael stands there quietly, looking embarrassed.

Ms. Davis: I'm disappointed in you, Michael. Do you have an explanation for this?

Michael: I'm sorry, Ms. Davis. It's a long story.

Ms. Davis: I'm listening.

Michael: I wasn't able to study. That's all.

Ms. Davis: Well, I'm sorry too.
(She puts the test in the trash can. Michael sits back down.)

Jennifer: Why didn't you tell Ms. Davis what happened?

Michael: It wouldn't matter. If I take the test, I fail. If I cheat, I fail. Either way, I fail.

Jennifer: But now she'll never trust you. She's really nice. Why don't you stay after class and explain to her why you didn't study? She knows you don't have to cheat to get a good grade.

Michael: I know she won't change my grade, but maybe she'll kind of understand why I did it.

Jennifer: I'm sorry, Michael. It was my idea for you to look at my paper.

Michael: It wasn't your fault. Don't worry about it. But I think I will stay and talk to Ms. Davis. I feel bad about what happened.

Jennifer: Good luck. I know Ms. Davis will listen and try to understand.

Michael: I hope you're right.

GA1689

To Cheat or Not to Cheat: That Is the Question

Discussion Questions

● Do you feel there are ever times when it's okay to cheat? Explain.

● How do you feel Ms. Davis should handle Michael's situation? Should she fail Michael, or do you feel she should give him another chance?

● Do you think Jennifer should be punished at all, or perhaps confide to Ms. Davis that she encouraged Michael to cheat?

● What suggestions could you give a teacher to keep students from cheating? (the types of tests given, seating arrangements, time allowed to study or prepare before a test)

● Let's pretend you cheated on a test, but did not get caught. Your guilty conscience continually haunts you. How would you handle this situation?

Extension Activities

● Review the following test-taking strategies with students. This will help them do the best they possibly can, no matter how prepared they are.

True/False Tests—Look for the words *such as, always, never, every,* and *all*. These words are clues that the statement or question is most likely not true. There are very few "absolutes" in the world.

Multiple-Choice Tests—Read every choice carefully. Cross off each choice you are sure is not correct. It is easier to make a selection when you have fewer answers to choose from. In addition, if the question ends in the word *an*, the answer must begin with a vowel!

Matching—Once again, read all the choices first. Match all those you're sure are correct. Then, go back and try to make intelligent choices matching those that remain.

Note: Refer students to the study/homework strategies presented after *The Dog Ate My Homework* on page 22.

● Ask students to role-play proper test taking. For example:

Student #1 sits open, with his test papers scattered on the desk. As he finishes one paper, the student places it out on the corner of the desk, wide open for all to see. He keeps arms at his sides, making no attempt to cover his paper.

Student #2 sits with her arms on each side of the desk, with the test papers in between her arms, one on top of the other. As the student finishes one paper, she places it under the pile and continues on to the next paper. She continues to keep her paper covered by leaving her arms resting on the desk on either side.

Invite the class to observe both students for several minutes as they role-play. Then ask them to share their observations. Ask students if they have any suggestions for improvement. Remind them that they can help each other to NOT cheat by eliminating the temptation.

Practice Makes Perfect

> ## Topic: Practicing an Instrument (During Your Free Time)!
>
> *Your students are now at the age when they begin taking lessons for musical instruments. However, though students begin these lessons with great enthusiasm, few think the decision through far enough to realize the responsibilities, dedication, and hard work involved. This play helps students discover what it really means to study an instrument or develop other skills such as dance, sports, drama, and so on, and the time and effort it takes to become proficient.*

Characters: Josh
His Mom

Setting: Living Room

Scene One

Josh has just returned home from school very enthused about starting lessons for a musical instrument.

Josh: Mom! Look! Mr. Taylor just passed out a paper about starting band lessons. I really want to play the drums, Mom. Can I?

Mom: Hold on, Josh, hold on. Let me read the paper first.

Mom takes the paper and looks it over.

Mom: What instrument are you interested in?

Josh: The drums, of course. That's the only thing worth playing!

Mom: I'm not so sure that's true, but if you feel that strongly about playing the drums I don't think I should even try to talk you into the trumpet, should I?

Josh: No way. I want to play the drums. Listen to this, I've already been practicing. *(Using his hands, Josh plays a beat on the table.)*

Mom: *(laughing)*
Okay, okay. I'll talk to your dad about it, but I don't see any problem with this.

Josh: Thanks, Mom! This is going to be great! I can't wait to start lessons.

Mom: If you do this, you will have to follow a practice schedule your father and I set up for you. You'll have to take this seriously, just like your school work.

Josh: I know. I'll practice every day. I promise.

Mom: *(looking a bit doubtful)*
I think those are the same words I heard from your sister three years ago when she started playing the flute. We all know how well that worked out.

Josh: I know, but I'm not her, Mom. She never sticks to anything she starts. I'll practice every day.

Scene Two
(Two Months Later)

Josh is sprawled on the couch watching TV. Mom enters the room.

Mom: Josh, it's time to practice your drum. I let you off yesterday because of baseball practice, but our deal was that you would make up the time today. Remember?

Josh: *(annoyed)*
I remember. Can't it wait until after this show?

Mom: No, it can't. We had a deal.
(She shuts off the television.)

Josh: Okay. It's just that playing drums is not what I expected. I have to use this stupid little pad instead of a real drum. How can I have fun playing drums on that thing?

Mom: Josh, you know your father and I agreed to buy you a snare drum if you stick to your lessons for at least six months. That's not much longer.

Josh: I know, but you have to admit that beating on that dumb piece of rubber is pretty boring.

Mom: *(smiling)*
I know my ears appreciate it.

Josh: Very funny.

Mom: I'm sorry, Josh. I think your enthusiasm for drum playing is starting to fade?

Josh: I didn't think it would, but like I said, I thought it would be more fun.

Mom: If you still really want to play the drums, I think you can stand four more months of the rubber pad. Everyone has to do it. Please give this some thought. Buying a real drum is a big investment. We need to have a commitment from you that you're going to stick with your lessons.

Josh: I do still want to play drums. I guess I just didn't realize how much work it was.

Mom: I think you can become really good if you keep taking lessons.

Josh: You're right. I have learned a lot. Thanks for the pep talk. I'm going to go practice right now.

Mom: That's what I was hoping you'd say.

Practice Makes Perfect

Discussion Questions

• Take a class survey of how many students play a musical instrument. How many take lessons in other things such as dance, gymnastics, ice-skating, and so on? How many play a sport of some kind? Hold a class discussion about everyone's interests.

• Did anyone take lessons for something they thought they would enjoy, only to find out they didn't? For those who have "stuck with it," what is it that keeps you dedicated? Do you feel pressure from your parents to continue, or do you truly enjoy the activity? If you didn't stick with it, what were your reasons for stopping?

• If you were allowed to take lessons for anything you wanted, what would you choose? Why?

• For those of you who have stuck with something for over a year, what is it about that activity that you enjoy and keeps you dedicated?

• How long do you feel someone should have to take lessons before being allowed to quit?

Extension Activities

• Invite students to conduct interviews with people who have "mastered" a craft, such as an instrument, singing, dancing, sport, and so on. Have students find out how many hours of practice (daily/weekly/monthly) these people put in to become "experts" in their fields. Have students graph results in class, and see, over a lifetime, how much time and dedication it takes to master a skill.

• Share the wide variety of special interests and hobbies students may want to pursue. There are lessons for painting, sign language, golf, drama, and so on, children can take through most community programs. Many children's

families can't afford to pay for lessons, so check your local Arts Institute, YMCA, or Boys/Girls Clubs for what is offered in your area. They may offer inexpensive or even free classes on special skills as well as a variety of sports programs. You may spark interests in your students that weren't there before!

• Ask students to work up a practice schedule for whatever it is they are learning. Make sure students understand that this can include any activity in which they are interested. It can be as simple as trying to improve hitting a softball or learning how to cook (because any activity in which we want to improve takes practice). Motivate students by offering a treat (e.g., free homework pass, candy, and so on) if they complete their chart for one month and return it to you with a parent signature.

• Hold a class talent show! Invite all willing students to prepare a presentation to perform for their classmates. You may even wish to invite other classes if you have enough participants. Give out rewards for Most Creative, Most Humorous, and so on, making sure you have a prize for all performing students. This is a great way to end the school year!

Not Making the Grade

> ## Topic: Grades Not as Good as Your Siblings
>
> *In today's fast-changing, competitive world, children are constantly being compared to others. Help students understand that even though they face competition with others in a number of situations, each person possesses special abilities and talents. Doing their best is what matters most.*

Characters: Terrance
His Mom and Dad

Setting: Living Room

Terrance enters the living room where Mom and Dad are sitting, reading.

Mom: Hi, Terrance.

Terrance: Hi. I'm starving, Mom. What's for supper?

Dad: There's some chicken in the oven. It'll be ready in about fifteen minutes.

Terrance: Great! Remember I have soccer tonight at six o'clock.

Dad: Good, you'll have enough time to eat with the family before I take you. I might even stay and watch awhile. The coach says you've really improved this year.

Terrance: I've been trying.

Mom: Do you have something to show us, Terrance?

Terrance: Like what?

Mom: Well, your sister had her report card today. She got straight A's, as always.

Terrance: Oh, yeah. I guess we did get those today.

Terrance sits down and begins to look through a magazine, ignoring his mother's comments.

Dad: Terrance, I think your mother wants to see your report card. Where is it?

Terrance: I think it's in my bookbag.
(He makes no move to get his report card.)

Mom: Okay, if you're not going to get it, I'll get it myself. I usually stay out of your bookbag, but obviously you're not planning on showing us how you did.

Terrance: No, I'll get it. I didn't know I had to get it out this minute.
(He gets out his report card.)

Mom: Easy, Terrance. I just wanted to see how you did. I didn't mean to get you upset. Is there a problem with your report card?

Terrance: A little bit. I just didn't do as well as I did last time, that's all. Here.
(He hands his mother the report card.)

Mom looks over the report card, then hands it to Dad.

Dad: I thought everything was okay. Why didn't you tell us you were having problems?

Mom: The papers I saw all looked good. If you got all C's and two D's on your report card, where are all the tests to show me this?

Terrance: *(looking at the floor)*
I didn't bring them home. I'm sorry.

Dad: I'm sorry you didn't feel you could come to us if you were having problems. I'm afraid soccer might have something to do with this.

Terrance: That's not true! Please, I know what you're going to say, and you can't take soccer away from me! It's the only thing I'm really good at.

Mom: You know that's not true. What do you suggest we do? Your grades are more important than soccer, and these grades aren't good enough. You can do much better than this.

Terrance: Well, I can't get straight A's like Kim. You always compare me to her, and I'll never do as well as her!
(He angrily leaves the room.)

Mom: Is Terrance right? Do I compare him to Kim? I certainly don't mean to.

Dad: Of course not. He is capable of doing much better with his grades. He might not be a straight A student, but he is certainly a B student.

Mom: Maybe we need to let him know we don't expect the same things from him that we expect from Kim. I don't want him to think Kim is smarter than he is.

Dad: We need to let Terrance know that we expect his best, and if his best is a B, or maybe a C once in a while, then we'll be satisfied.

Mom: I guess our children have their own talents. But we need Terrance to know that soccer cannot get in the way of school. He's always been a good student.

Dad: Let's go talk to him. I'm sure we can make him feel better, and then we'll set up a plan to get these grades up.

Not Making the Grade

Discussion Questions

- Do you feel Terrance's parents are understanding? Do you have any suggestions for how they can help Terrance? What might Terrance have to do if his parents weren't quite as supportive?

- Do you ever feel as though you are compared to your siblings by your parents? teachers? friends? How can you approach your parents and/or teachers to discuss this topic?

- Do you understand how easy it is for parents to compare their children, even if they try not to? Do you ever compare your parents and the way they discipline you? Is it fair for you to compare your parents to each other, or compare them to your friends' parents? Why are comparisons like this unfair?

- Comparisons between siblings, friends, classmates, teammates, and so on, occur every day in many situations. Can you think of times when comparisons have positive results?

- What do you think this statement means? *When striving for success, compete only with yourself.*

- Terrance seems to have trouble balancing sports and academics. If you are involved in sports or any other extracurricular activities, do these activities ever affect your grades? How? How is it possible to balance other activities with school work? Share your strategies with the class.

Extension Activities

- Ask students to make a chart listing their brothers, sisters, and any other people to whom they feel compared. Then have them add themselves to the chart. Students should write down every area in which these people excel, as well as the areas in which they themselves excel. Charting people's talents as well as their own helps students see that everyone has areas of great ability. When students find themselves feeling jealous towards siblings or friends, it's rewarding to remind themselves that they possess talents and abilities of their own.

- Pair up students with classmates. Ask each pair to create a Venn diagram, comparing each other. When finished, students may share what they learned about each other with the class. Did you learn something new or interesting about your partner? Did you discover hidden talents? This is a great way for students to get to know and appreciate each other on a different level.

GA1689

No One Will Ever Know

Topic: Whether or Not to Return Lost Money You Find

Everyone has a good and bad conscience that speaks to us when we try to make decisions. Sometimes we lend a deaf ear to our good conscience because our bad conscience might be easier to listen to. This play helps students understand that while they may never be caught doing something wrong, they will always have to live with the decisions they make.

Characters: Jason
Good Conscience
Bad Conscience

Setting: Along the Sidewalk

Jason is on his way to the park to play basketball with his friends when he suddenly sees a twenty-dollar bill on the sidewalk.

Jason: What's this?
(He bends down to pick up the bill.)
A twenty-dollar bill! I could really use this!
(He looks around anxiously to see if anyone saw him pick up the money.)

Bad Conscience: Good! Nobody saw you. You can keep it and no one will ever know.

Jason: Should I do that?

Bad Conscience: Sure, why not? You could buy that new football jersey you've been wanting.

Good Conscience: Be quiet, B.C.! Jason, you know better than that. Look! There's a man in a suit over there who's looking for something by that bench. Go ask him what he's looking for.

Jason: I could at least do that. If he doesn't say "money," then I'll know this isn't his, and I won't have to feel guilty about keeping it.

Good Conscience: That's right, Jason. I knew I could count on you to do the right thing!

Bad Conscience: You're crazy, Jason! That man is probably looking for his dog or something. How would he ever notice if he lost a twenty-dollar bill? People don't feel money fall out of their pockets. Keep it! No one will ever know!

Jason: I don't know what to do. Would both of you quit talking to me? I'm getting confused!

Good Conscience: Just go ask the man, Jason.

Bad Conscience: Go the other way, Jason. Take the money to the park and buy your friends some soda. Then you won't even pass the man. If you don't pass him, you won't need to talk to him.

Good Conscience: You'll never be able to live with yourself if you listen to him, Jason. You're a good and honest person, and I know you'll do the right thing.

Jason: But I don't even know that man. I'm going to feel stupid going up and talking to him. Besides, I'm not supposed to talk to strangers.

Bad Conscience: That's right! Now you're talking. Your mother would be furious with you if you approached a stranger.

Good Conscience: Jason, the man is with his wife and two little children. How dangerous could that be? He probably met them on his lunch hour. With two children, I'm sure they can use that twenty dollars.

Jason: Okay, okay, I'll just go up to him real quick.

Bad Conscience: You'll be sorry, Jason.

Jason: No, I'll be sorry if I don't find out the truth about this twenty-dollar bill.

Good Conscience: I'm proud of you, Jason. Just think of how you would feel if you were the one who lost that money. Wouldn't you want someone to return it to you?

Jason: Yes, I would.

Bad Conscience: But it's not you. "Finders keepers," as the saying goes.

Jason: No, I think I'm going to ask that man if this belongs to him. If it doesn't, then I can keep it and not feel bad about it.

Good Conscience: Good job, Jason! Let's go.

Jason walks over towards the man, with Good Conscience following.

Bad Conscience: Don't worry, Goody Two Shoes. I'll win next time.

No One Will Ever Know

Discussion Questions

• Share times when you've struggled with your good and bad conscience. Did you find something that didn't belong to you? Did someone give you too much change? Did you want to lie about something so you wouldn't get in trouble? What did you do, and how do you feel about what you did?

• Is there ever a time when you feel it's okay to keep something that's been lost?

• What would you have done if you were in Jason's situation? Why?

• When your good and bad conscience are battling with each other, it often helps to talk about the situation with another person, perhaps a teacher, friend, or parent. With whom do you feel most comfortable discussing your problems and concerns?

• Do you believe people really have a good and bad conscience? If so, do you think they are helpful or annoying? Explain.

Extension Activities

• Ask students to write letters to an imaginary advice columnist—you can create the name! Have students write about a "sticky" or problematic situation over which their good and bad conscience are wrestling. Invite students to ask the columnist for advice, and sign their names in fun, creative ways, such as *Troubled in Toronto* or *Seeking Help in Helena*. After each student has written a letter, collect the papers and pass them out randomly to the class. Now it is time for students to offer advice to their classmates! Students may create small groups, read the letters aloud, and then come up with consensus replies and advice, or write letters of advice back to the writers.

• When people begin to listen to their good conscience and follow its advice, this person is showing maturity and growth. Brainstorm with students a list of behaviors that demonstrate maturity. Invite them to provide real or made-up situations in which these behaviors might occur.

• Using some of the ideas students brainstormed, have the class break up into small groups and write short skits similar to *No One Will Ever Know*, demonstrating various situations in which one struggles with his or her good and bad conscience. Invite groups to present their skits to the class, and then discuss the outcomes.

Moms Aren't Allowed to Get Sick!

Topic: Appreciating Parents and Friends

Sometimes we take the people who mean the most to us for granted. In this play, students reflect upon the special people in their lives, and all that they do for them. The character of Wendy finds her mother suddenly sick in the hospital and realizes, by her absence, how much her mother does for her and the family. The play also promotes discussion of how we can show the special people in our lives how much we appreciate them.

Characters: Wendy, Toby, and Tham (friends from school)

Setting: Sidewalk Next to School

Wendy, Toby, and Tham are walking home from school. Wendy looks a little depressed, so her friends try to cheer her up.

Wendy: I wish I could go skating. My dad said I have to go straight home after school. Old Mrs. Wharton is baby-sitting us, and Dad doesn't want me out of the house while she's there.

Toby: My mom would be willing to give you a ride if that's the problem, Wendy. We practically go right by your house.

Wendy: I wish that were the only problem, but like I said, it really has nothing to do with needing a ride. Dad just said that since he has to be at the hospital to visit Mom, he feels better when he knows I'm safe at home.

Tham: He probably doesn't want to worry about any accidents happening. One member of the family in the hospital at a time is enough.

Wendy: I guess you're right. I never realized everything my mom did for me until she got sick. Last night we ate hot dogs for the third time in a row. Tonight Dad promised he'd make something different.

Toby: Is Mrs. Wharton nice?

Wendy: She tries, but she doesn't let me watch half of the shows my mom and dad let me watch. And she doesn't let me stay on the phone very long.

Toby: Why don't you ask your dad to talk to her?

Wendy: I already did. He said to try and just put up with it for a little while. He doesn't want to "rock the boat" when Mrs. Wharton is the only sitter he can find.

Tham: Hey, maybe tomorrow you could come to my house. That would give you a little break from Mrs. Wharton.

Wendy: Thanks, Tham, but I might get to visit my mom tomorrow night. I'll ask my dad about it for the next night, though, okay?

Tham: Good. I'll get my mom to take us out for pizza!

Wendy: Would you? That would be great!

Toby: And I'll ask if you can come to my house the next night.

Wendy: This is great! If I can hang out at both of your houses until my mom is better maybe it won't be so bad.

Toby: Hey, let's all wear our team shirts to school tomorrow. I'll call some of the other girls and try and get everyone to wear them.

Wendy: Uhh . . . I don't think so. Mine is still caked with mud from the slide I took in last week's game. No one has done the wash since Mom went to the hospital. Between his job and trying to spend time at the hospital, my dad hasn't had time. I guess I never realized how much my mom does for me.

Toby: Why don't Tham and I come over and help you do the wash? It can't be that hard. My brother even throws some clothes in now and then.

Wendy: But he's a lot older than us.

Tham: I know, but we do know how to read, and the difference between dark and white clothes. All you have to do is separate the colors. Come on, we'll help you, and we can always call my mom if we have a problem.

Toby: Or I'm sure Mrs. Wharton can help us.

Wendy: Well, okay. I never realized how much stuff my mom takes care of at our house. I even miss her bugging me to finish my homework. I guess good things can come from bad things. Thanks a lot, you guys.

Tham: Any time.

Toby: If you can't count on your family and friends, who can you count on?

The three girls walk off to Wendy's house to start on the laundry.

Moms Aren't Allowed to Get Sick!

Discussion Questions

- Take a minute to think about everything your parents/guardians do for you. Share your thoughts with the class.

- Brainstorm all the ways you do and can help your parents/guardians around the house. Do you try to help out more if a parent is sick or extra busy with work?

- Think about your friends. What qualities make a good friend? If your friend was in the same situation as Wendy, how could you help?

- Are there other people in your life who help you in special ways (maybe a teacher, minister/youth leader, relative, neighbor, or a friend's mother and father)? Share stories about the times these special people helped you in some way.

- What do you think this statement means? *Life is all about giving. This, not material wealth, will make you rich.*

Extension Activities

- Invite students to create a bulletin-board display about the special people in their lives. Have each student bring in a photo or draw a picture of someone who is special to him or her. Students can write acrostic poems with that person's name, for example, *KATIE: K–kind, A–always listens, T–tons of fun!, I–interesting, E–exciting to be with!* They can also write a short paragraph telling why this person is so special. Attach student writing and photos to the bulletin board.

- Invite each student to make a card of appreciation for a person who does a lot for him or her. Inside the card, have students write down all the things they appreciate about this person, and how he or she plays a special role in their lives.

- Have students create five "I.O.U. Coupons" to give to people they appreciate. The coupons can be for household chores, outdoor chores, helping with younger siblings or pets, and so on. Encourage students to be creative and think of specific chores or activities these special people will appreciate. Coupons make great gifts for Mother's and Father's Day!

GA1689

You're Wearing THAT?

> ## Topic: Choosing Your Own Style
>
> *Students love talking about the types of clothes and styles they like and what types they don't. Help students realize that clothes make an impression upon others about what type of person we are. This play is a fun way to introduce discussion on styles of the past and present, and how clothes often reflect our personalities. Note: This play can be changed, or updated, to accommodate whatever fashions or styles are currently "trendy."*

Characters: Nicole (age 11) and Chris (age 10); brother and sister
Their Mom and Dad

Setting: Living Room

The family is getting ready to go to the local high school's Friday night football game. Mom and Dad are waiting for Nicole and Chris.

Dad: Are the kids almost ready? We're going to miss the opening kickoff.

Mom: I'm sure we'll be there in plenty of time. The game doesn't start until eight o'clock.

Dad: It's seven-thirty! Let's go, Nicole! Come on, Chris!

Nicole: *(from offstage)*
We're coming!

Nicole and Chris enter dressed in baggy shirts and pants.

Dad: Just what is that you're wearing? It looks like you got into my closet and put on my clothes!

Chris: Dad! Believe me, I'm not wearing your clothes. I'm sure. And these fit perfectly fine. I just bought these clothes today.

Nicole: Me too. Mom took us to the mall and we both got new clothes. I guess I should say thank you to you too.
(She gives her dad a hug.)
Thanks, Dad.

Dad: *(looking at Mom in disbelief)*
You bought these clothes for them? What were you thinking?

Mom: I don't know what you mean.

Dad: How can you not know what I mean? These clothes are falling off of them! One tug and Chris's pants will be down around his ankles.

Mom: Oh, honey, all the kids are wearing clothes like this.

Chris: Come on, Dad. Don't make such a big deal out of it. We're going to be late for the game, right? Opening kickoff is in twenty minutes.

Dad: Well, I guess I'm going to miss it then, because I'm not taking my children to a football game dressed like this.

Mom: Don't be silly! They look fine.

Dad: I want you two to go upstairs right now and put on some pants that fasten above your hips, and shirts that don't hang down to your knees!

Nicole: Dad, please! Chris and I look fine.

Dad: You look like a boy, Nicole.

Nicole: I do not. I'm just wearing normal clothes.

Dad: I just want you to look like normal kids. Is there something wrong with that?

Mom: But they do look like normal kids. This is what they dress like now. When is the last time you went clothes shopping with them? Clothes have changed a lot in the past few years.

Dad: Not that much.

Mom: Try to remember what it was like when we were kids. Our parents didn't exactly approve of what we wore all the time. They just want to dress like everyone else.

Chris: Come on, tell us what you wore when you were our age, Dad.

Chris and Nicole laugh, and Mom smiles.

Dad: *(rolling his eyes)*
Okay, okay, forget it. Let's go to the game.

Behind Dad's back, the kids and Mom give each other big grins as they leave for the game.

You're Wearing THAT?

Discussion Questions

- What are some of today's styles? Can you think of styles that have already been "in" and "out" during your lifetime? Share some of the styles you like and dislike. (It's always a lot of fun for you to also share some of the styles you wore as a child and teenager.)

- How does fashion create a certain impression on others? Do you think people dress to make an impression on others, or only to please themselves?

- How important is it to you to wear designer clothes? Would it bother you if one of your friends didn't wear designer clothing? How much money could you save if you were willing to wear tennis shoes or jeans that are a quality brand, but not "the" brand everyone else is wearing?

- How do you dress differently for various activities or events, such as a football game? dance? church? school? shopping? movies? around the house? Why do you dress the way you do for these situations?

- What are the pros and cons of wearing school uniforms? Share your opinions and feelings. Why do some people think school uniforms should be required? Do you agree or disagree with these opinions? Why? Do you think wearing different kinds of clothes to school is an important part of self expression? Should there be ANY rules or restrictions about what should not be worn to school?

Extension Activities

- Hold a "designer" session in class. Ask each student to design and draw a picture of a style that expresses his or her own taste in clothing. Have students share their designs with the class and explain why they like these styles. Display students' drawings on a bulletin board titled *Our Class Has Style!* As an extension, students can design what they consider to be the UGLIEST outfit ever! Encourage them to be as creative as possible, and explain why they would never let their own children wear these styles.

- Invite children to interview their parents and other adults about how they dressed as children and teenagers. Have each student come back with one story to share with the class about the reactions these people received from parents and/or other people regarding their clothing and hairstyles.

- Create a "fashion display." Ask students to bring in pictures of themselves when they were younger and wearing a variety of different styles. Bring in pictures of yourself (if you're not too embarrassed!) as well, at a variety of ages, wearing different fashions and hairstyles. Children will love seeing these pictures! Also invite them to bring in pictures of their parents, siblings, and grandparents, so they can see how fashions and hairstyles change over time, and even come back in fashion!

GA1689

Naughty Notes

Characters: Cara and Lin (friends and classmates)
Mr. Simms (their teacher)
Several other students (non-speaking parts)

Setting: Classroom, During a Lesson

All students are sitting in class, while Mr. Simms delivers a boring lecture about the digestive system. They are staring blankly ahead of them or falling asleep.

Mr. Simms: *(in a monotone, drawling voice)*
Students, for the last part of class we want to take a trip—a trip through our bodies. Who knows what this path is called?

The students look blankly back at Mr. Simms.

Mr. Simms: Now class, we learned this yesterday. Let me give you a hint.
(He pushes his glasses up off his nose.)
It begins with a D.

The students still stare back blankly, and one yawns.

Mr. Simms: *(sarcastically)*
Okay, I can see so much of what I'm teaching you is sticking in your brains. Everyone repeat after me . . . "the digestive system."

Class: *(in bored voices)*
The digestive system.

As Mr. Simms continues speaking, Cara passes a note to Lin.

Mr. Simms: Good, good. When we eat, our food it travels from our mouths, down our throats, and then into our stomachs.

Cara: Mr. Simms?

Mr. Simms: Yes, Cara? Do you have a question?

Cara: What happens to our food when we throw it up?

The students laugh.

Mr. Simms: If I thought you were serious, Cara, I might actually answer your question.

Lin passes a note back to Cara.

Mr. Simms: May I have that please, Cara?

Cara hands Mr. Simms the pencil she is holding in her hand.

Cara: Sure, Mr. Simms, you can borrow it. I have an extra in my notebook.

Mr. Simms: Not your pencil, Cara. I would like the note Lin just passed to you while I was trying to teach.

Cara: What note? I don't know what you're talking about, Mr. Simms.

Mr. Simms: Lin?

Lin: Oh, that? That wasn't a note.

Mr. Simms: What exactly was it then, Lin?

Lin: Umm . . . it had notes from class on it, and I borrowed it from Cara yesterday since I wasn't here. I was just giving them back to her.

Mr. Simms: I see . . . Well, then, you won't mind if I take a look at the notes. I certainly want to make sure Cara gave you all the information you missed from yesterday's class.

Mr. Simms takes the note from Cara and opens it.

Mr. Simms: I guess these are notes from yesterday.
(He turns the paper over. His eyes pop open in shock.)
Well! I want both of you girls to stay after class. I don't care how bored you get in my classroom, I certainly don't deserve this!

Lin/Cara: Yes, Mr. Simms.

The bell rings.

Cara: I guess we're in trouble now.

Lin: Yeah, great. Do you think he'll send us to the principal's office?

Cara: I hope not!

As the other students get up to leave, the girls sit with Mr. Simms, awaiting their punishment.

51

Naughty Notes

Discussion Questions

● Assuming that what Lin and Cara were writing about Mr. Simms was rather nasty, what punishment do you think they should receive?

● How many of you write notes to your friends during class? Do you think it's fair for you to be punished when you are caught? Explain.

● When during the school day do you think it should be okay to write notes to your friends? (before class, free time, lunchtime, recess)

● Usually students write notes in class because something has happened that seems far more important than the class material being taught. However, besides getting caught, what other negative results may come from note writing in class?

● When is note writing a good thing? (when you are thanking somebody, to cheer someone up, to say you're sorry, to congratulate someone)

Extension Activities

● Hold a note-writing session for writing practice. Allow students to sit by friends and engage in written conversations. While they're having fun writing notes back and forth to each other, they must keep in mind your objectives—using complete sentences, proper capitalization, punctuation, and so on.

● Invite student groups to write their own endings to the play. What punishment do students think Cara and Lin should receive from Mr. Simms? Did Lin and Cara apologize? Did they continue writing notes even after they were told not to? After students have written their endings, invite them to perform their skits for the class.

● Invite students to write a thoughtful note to one of their teachers, now or in the past. Students can write why they enjoyed having this person as a teacher, maybe something special they learned in this person's class, or a special experience this teacher provided. Deliver the notes for children. Teachers enjoy a note of appreciation or thanks now and then!

Tag-Along Troubles

Topic: A Younger Sibling Who Always Wants to "Tag Along"

All of us have probably "tagged along" at one time or another, whether with a brother/sister or a friend. This play gives students the chance to voice their feelings about siblings tagging along, and how it feels to want to tag along with others. It also promotes discussion on how students can be sensitive to the feelings of older and younger siblings and/or friends, when it's okay to want to be on their own, and when they should try to include others.

Characters: Mateo (age 11) and Brett (age 8); brothers
Their Mom

Setting: Front Yard

Mateo and his little brother, Brett, have just finished playing catch. Mateo now wants to go to his friend's house, but without Brett tagging along.

Mateo: Okay, Brett, let's call it quits. We've been out here half an hour.

Brett: Okay, what do you want to do now?

Mateo: I told Jeff I was coming over.

Brett: Can I come? Can I? Please?

Mateo: Brett, I just played ball with you. Can't I go places without you sometimes?

Brett: Mom! Can I go with Mateo to Jeff's house?

Mom: *(calling out from the house)*
Sure, honey. Just make sure you're back in time for dinner.

Mateo: Mom! I didn't invite Brett to come!

Mom comes to the door.

Mom: What's going on out here?

Mateo: Mom, I didn't invite Brett to come with me. Can't I please go somewhere without him? I'm not trying to be mean, but I have to take him everywhere with me. Please let me go to Jeff's by myself.

Mom: Brett, can't you just stay here with me?

53   GA1689

Brett:	Nooooo! There's nothing to do here!
Mateo:	Please, Mom!
Mom:	Go on, Mateo. You've already spent a lot of time with Brett this morning. Brett, come inside and we'll find something for you to do.
Brett:	But I'm bored! I like going to Jeff's house.
Mateo:	Mom, I've been home with Brett practically all day.
Mom:	Mateo's right, Brett. Sometimes your brother likes to do things on his own. We'll find something fun to do here, okay? You go on to Jeff's house, Mateo.
Mateo:	Thanks, Mom. *(He heads off towards Jeff's house.)*
Brett:	*(calling after Mateo)* Don't ask me to play with you when you get home then!
Mateo:	Fine!
Brett:	Fine!
Mom:	Brett, you have to realize that Mateo needs time by himself with his friends, too. Why don't you call a friend over, and then you'll have something to do.
Brett:	You don't care?
Mom:	Of course not. Let's see who we can call.
Brett:	Thanks, Mom.
Mom:	You're welcome. But the next time this happens, I don't want to see this behavior again. Am I understood?
Brett:	Understood.
Mom:	Good.

Mom and Brett go into the house.

Tag-Along Troubles

Discussion Questions

● Most siblings deal with this situation from time to time. We know that often little brothers and sisters look up to us and enjoy spending time with us and our friends. Does this scene sound familiar to some of you? How is this situation handled in your own families?

● Share some of the activities you enjoy doing with your brothers/sisters. Then share some activities you would rather do on your own. Why is it important for you to have time to yourself and with your friends?

● Do any of you get paid to watch a younger brother/sister? When do you feel you should be paid for spending time with your siblings, and when is this just the responsibility of being part of a family?

● Are any of you the younger siblings in the family? Have you ever wanted to "tag along" with older brothers or sisters when you thought they were doing something fun? Share how it feels to be the younger sibling. Do you feel you should always be included in your older brothers'/sisters' activities? Explain.

● How many of you are "only children"? Do you ever wish you had a sibling? If so, what is it about having siblings that makes you want them? Those of you who have siblings, please share the pros and cons of having brothers and/or sisters.

My Little Brother, Brett

Brett is fun to be with because he is funny and sweet. He always lets me read to him, and he helps me clean my room.

Extension Activities

● Ask students to draw a picture of themselves doing a favorite activity with their siblings. If they have no siblings, they can draw a picture with their pet, a cousin, or other family member. They can also bring in a favorite photograph to share. Then invite each student to share with the class why this particular sibling/pet/parent is important to them, or a funny incident or story.

● Hold a "Bring Your Sibling to Lunch Day" at school. If a student's brother or sister is already in the same school, this may be easily arranged. Otherwise, perhaps some parents would be willing to drive siblings to school for lunch, and the parents may stay as well. Students are often able to arrange this if the district's elementary, middle, and high schools are near each other. Encourage "only children" to invite a favorite cousin, friend, or other family member.

Where Do You Shop? A Thrift Store?

> ## Topic: Judging on Appearances
> ## (Making Fun of Someone's Clothes)
>
> *Not everyone can afford designer clothing. Students who can, however, are sometimes less than understanding and sympathetic of those who can't. This play shows students how painful it can be to be judged by others, as well as help them learn to accept others, whether or not their clothes or appearance is similar to their own.*

Characters: Jenna and Huma (best friends)
Lauren (their classmate)

Setting: Lunch Tables at School

Lauren is standing in the lunch line, close by where Huma and Jenna are sitting at a table eating lunch.

Huma: I love your new haircut, Jenna. I can't wait to get mine done this Friday.

Jenna: Your hair is going to look so cute. I wish I could come with you. I can't believe you're finally cutting your long hair. I love your hair, but it's going to look great cut shorter.

Huma: I hope so. I'm going shopping right after my haircut. My mom said I could get some new sandals for summer.

Jenna: I'm getting some, too. My old ones are all worn out.

Huma suddenly spots Lauren standing in line. She nudges Jenna to look, and they both whisper to each other and try not to laugh. Lauren's shoes are old and worn out, nothing like what Huma and Jenna would wear.

Jenna: *(trying to whisper)*
Talk about being all worn out. Look at Lauren. Can you believe she comes to school like that?

Huma: I would refuse to come to school if my parents made me wear those clothes.

Jenna: They must be able to afford something better than that. And look at her shoes. Weren't those in style like five years ago or something?

Huma: Maybe she just doesn't care what she looks like. It looks like she buys her clothes at a thrift store.

Jenna: Yeah, like the Salvation Army.
(The girls laugh.)

Lauren, who has overheard everything Huma and Jenna have been saying, suddenly turns and walks over to them.

Lauren: I heard every word you both said.

Jenna: *(embarrassed)*
We weren't talking about you, Lauren.

Lauren: You were so, Jenna. I am so tired of the both of you looking down on everybody. You act so high and mighty, as if you're better than everyone else just because you have the best of everything.

Huma: You don't have to get so upset, Lauren.

Lauren: And you wouldn't?

Huma: Maybe you shouldn't be listening in on other people's conversations.

Lauren: By the way, Jenna, my outfit *is* from the Salvation Army, and I'm proud of it. My mom worked long and hard just so she had a few extra dollars for me to have this outfit. You two have no idea what it's like to need things. You get everything you want without even thinking about it.

Jenna: I don't always get everything I want.

Lauren: Well, you just don't know what it's like to not have money. Maybe my clothes aren't as nice as yours, but I like them just fine.

Jenna: I'm sorry, Lauren.

Huma: We don't have to take this from you, you know.

Lauren: No, Huma, *I* don't have to take this from *you.*

Lauren walks away with her head held high, while Huma and Jenna are left looking at each other, wondering what to say.

Where Do You Shop? A Thrift Store?

Discussion Questions

- Lauren talked about "needing" things, and also about "wanting" things. What's the difference between "needs" and "wants"? For example, you may *want* a new bike, but you *need* new shoes if the old ones are worn out.

- Come up with several descriptive words describing each character in the play. Which character do you like the best? Which character is most like you?

- If you overheard the conversation in this play, what would you do? Would you defend Lauren? How might you help her feel better about her situation?

- Have you ever found yourselves gossiping or talking behind someone's back without really knowing this person's situation? If you knew the situation, how might your opinions change? (Give examples, such as if someone can't afford to buy nice clothes because his or her parent lost a job.)

- How do you feel about wearing "hand-me-downs" from older siblings, cousins, and so on? What do you do with clothes you outgrow?

- Years ago, most kids thought it was embarrassing to shop at a thrift store, but now lots of kids enjoy what we now call "vintage clothing." How would you feel about shopping at a second-hand store? What kinds of fun and interesting things can you find there?

Extension Activities

- Hold a clothing drive for a local rescue mission or the Red Cross. It's fun to have students do this as a group project. Ask each group to design a large paper doll. For every article of clothing they bring in, they are allowed to add a piece of clothing to their paper doll. The first group who dresses their doll may win candy, free time, a homework pass, or another treat. Make sure to reward everyone who brings in clothes.

- Have students make lists of their needs and wants. How do they differentiate between the two? Invite them to share several items from their lists with the rest of the class, explaining why they placed each item in its respective category.

- Ask student groups to add another character to the play, someone who may change the story line and/or the outcome. Invite them to write an extension to the play and present it to the rest of the class.

Shadow's Gone

> ## Topic: Dealing with the Death of a Pet
>
> *Dealing with the death of a pet is difficult at any age. Pets who have been around a long time become family members and friends. This play creates the opportunity for students to talk about their pets, and what they mean to them. It also invites students to talk about their experiences with losing pets, and how they and their families got through this difficult time.*

Characters: Rick
His Dad

Setting: Scene 1—Dining Room
Scene 2—Rick's Bedroom

Scene One

Rick and his dad are sitting at the dining-room table together eating an after-school snack.

Dad: How was school today, Rick?

Rick: Same as usual. Nothing really great happened.

Dad: I thought you were setting rockets off for your science project this week. What happened?

Rick: Oh, yeah. It was too windy, so we're doing that tomorrow. I can't wait to set off those rockets. Mine is going to be great. I practiced setting it off last Friday, and it went so far that Shadow had to run and fetch it for me.

Dad: He's able to do that?

Rick: Yeah, you should have seen him. He sat there watching the rocket go up, and then, as soon as the parachute went off, he started running towards the rocket.

Dad: *(laughing a little)*
I'm sorry I missed that. Shadow is quite a dog. He's been around a long time.

Rick: As long as I can remember.

Dad: That's because your mom and I bought Shadow before you were even born. I guess you might say Shadow was our first "baby."

Rick:		So who was easier to raise, Shadow or me? *(They laugh.)*
Dad:		I think we both know the answer to that. *(He suddenly becomes more serious.)* I do have some news to share with you about Shadow.
Rick:		What's that?
Dad:		When I came home at lunch today, he was having a lot of trouble breathing. I took him to the vet, and that's where he is right now.
Rick:		*(very concerned)* Is he going to be okay?
Dad:		We don't know. The doctor is running some tests and she's going to call me later.
Rick:		*(obviously upset)* I'm going to do my homework.
Dad:		I'm sorry, Rick. Hopefully the news will be good when the doctor calls.

Rick heads to his bedroom, not answering. Dad looks after him, worried.

Scene Two

The phone rings, and Dad answers.

Dad: Hello? . . . Yes, doctor . . . I see . . . Okay . . . We'll be right there.

Dad hangs up the phone and goes to Rick's room. He knocks on the door.

Rick: Come in.

Dad: Rick, that was the doctor on the phone. She wants us to come down to the animal hospital. Shadow's not in very good shape, Rick. I think we may have to put him down.

Rick: No, Dad! He was fine the other day!

Dad: I'm sorry, Rick, but we have to. The doctor said he's in a lot of pain.

Rick buries his head in his pillow. Dad puts his hand on Rick's shoulder.

Dad: I'm so sorry. I'm going to miss him, too.

Rick: I want to go see him.

Dad: Okay. I told the doctor we'd be right there. Let's go tell Shadow good-bye.

Shadow's Gone

Discussion Questions

● Dogs and other animals can truly can be some of our best friends and family members. Share some stories about your pets or other animals you've been close to.

● Losing a pet is never easy. Some people consider their pets as members of their family. Have any of you experienced the loss of a pet? How were you able to get over the loss? Share how you and your family handled this together.

● Some pet owners hold funeral services for their pets. Have any of you done this? Share your experiences with the class.

● For some people, getting over the loss of a pet is easier if they get a new pet right away. Others can't even think about another pet because of the sorrow they feel after losing their treasured friend. What do you think is the best way to handle such a loss?

● Talk about unusual animals people have as pets (e.g., snakes, iguanas, chameleons, pot-bellied pigs). Can these pets become as close to someone as domesticated animals like dogs and cats?

● Why do you think pets make such great companions and friends?

● Do you think there's any truth to the idea that dog owners start to look like their dogs?

Extension Activities

● Have each student write a short essay sharing their understanding of the saying: *Dog is man's (or woman's) best friend,* and then compare it to how they feel about their own or someone else's pet. When students' essays are complete, post them on a bulletin board titled *Pets Make Forever Friends.* Invite students to bring in photos or draw pictures of these animals and post them next to their essays.

● Have a class Pet Show! Principals tend to shy away from pets coming to school, but if it's at all possible, see if you can "swing" it. Students love animal visits at school. If you're not able to have pets at school, ask students to videotape or bring in photos of their pets and share them during a special time set aside during class. Invite students without pets to draw or cut out a picture of a pet they would like to have, or another animal they are close to.

● Have students create their very own unique pets from cutouts and drawings of various animal parts. Have them glue cutouts to construction paper and add a short description of the animal, including its name, all the funny and crazy things it can do, the sounds it makes, and why it is such a great pet!

 GA1689

Help! My Parents Are Getting a Divorce!

> ## Topic: Coping with Divorce
>
> *With so many families experiencing divorce today, sometimes it helps students to realize they are not alone. Whether students are dealing with a divorce in their immediate family, extended family, or with friends, they should learn where and how to seek support, as well as how they can help and support others.*

Characters: Alison and Connie (best friends)
Mrs. Baker (Connie's mother)

Setting: Alison's Dining Room; Connie's Kitchen

The play begins at Alison's house as she arrives home after school.

Alison: Finally! I thought today would never end!
(She tosses her bookbag on a chair and begins looking for something to eat in the refrigerator.)
I'm starving! Let's see . . . leftover noodles . . . and something with green gunk growing all over it . . . gross!

Alison spots a basket of fresh fruit on the dining-room table and smiles as she picks up an apple. She notices a sheet of paper on the table.

Alison: What's this?
(She picks up the paper and begins reading it.)
Oh, my gosh!
(She continues reading.)
This can't be true! It has to be some kind of a joke!

Alison sits down, obviously upset and confused.

Alison: This can't be right. I've got to call Connie.

Alison picks up the phone and dials Connie's number. The phone rings at Connie's house, and Connie's mother answers.

Mrs. Baker: Hello?

Alison: Hi, Mrs. Baker. Is Connie there?

Mrs. Baker: Alison, I'm sorry dear, but how many times must I ask you not to call Connie at dinner time?

Alison: Please, Mrs. Baker, I'm sorry. I just really need to talk to her.

Mrs. Baker: Five minutes, Alison.
(She covers the receiver with her hand.)
Connie! Alison's on the phone!

Connie runs over to the phone.

Mrs. Baker: I told her we were just sitting down to dinner, but she insists she needs to talk to you right now. What's wrong? Did her boyfriend break up with her again?

Connie: *(covering the receiver)*
Mom!

Mrs. Baker holds up her finger and mouths "five minutes" to Connie.

Connie: Hi, Ali. What's up?

Alison: You're not going to believe this, Connie. I found this paper on our table. It has to be some kind of a joke—it has to be!

Connie: What are you talking about?

Alison: I found a paper on the dining-room table. It's some kind of legal thing and it says "Divorce Decree" at the top.

Connie: What else does it say?

Alison: It has my parents' names on it—Donna T. Stone versus Howard M. Stone. Then it says a whole bunch of stuff I don't understand.

Connie: Try and relax, Alison. Just calm down.

Alison: What should I do? How could my parents do this to me?

Mrs. Baker: Your five minutes are up, Connie.

Connie: Listen, Ali, will you be okay until after dinner? You know how my mom is.

Alison: I don't know. I feel sick. If they were really going to get a divorce, wouldn't they tell me? How could they not tell me?

Mrs. Baker: When I said five minutes, I meant five minutes. Dinner is ready.

Connie: *(nodding to her mother)*
It's going to be okay, Ali.

Alison: How are you so sure? Connie, tell me what to do! I don't know what to do!

Connie: I'll talk to my mom. I have to go; I'm sorry. I'll call you back right after dinner.

Alison: Okay. But please call me back as soon as you're done.

Connie: I will. I promise.

GA1689

Help! My Parents Are Getting a Divorce!

Discussion Questions

- What do you think Connie should do to help her friend Alison now and in the future? What have you done to help a friend or sibling during a divorce?

- What changes do you think arise in a family after a divorce?

- Are any of you willing to share ways your family makes a divorce situation work? How did you learn to accept and work with the situation? Please share any suggestions you may have.

- Fairy tales always end with "happily ever after." We know real life can't always be like a fairy tale, and that relationships aren't always easy. It takes a lot of work to maintain a happy, long-lasting relationship. What are some of the important things people need to do to have a happy relationship?

- It's important to understand that parents are human, and they're not perfect. Divorce is a painful time for everyone in the family. Rather than being bitter towards your parents about a divorce, how can you help them? How can you make things easier during this difficult time?

Extension Activities

- In small groups, invite students to create several possible endings to the play. They may wish to show Alison seeking help from an adult, or possibly confronting her parents about what she's learned. They can also show how Connie can help Alison. Encourage students to perform their play endings for classmates.

- Ask students to write about how they feel when faced with a difficult situation. This situation doesn't have to be a divorce in their family, although it could be. Problems can include: fighting among siblings, a death in the family, moving, and so on. Ask students to include an explanation of the problem or situation, from whom they sought advice, and how they solved the problem. If students are willing, ask them to share their writing with the class.